Hustling and Bustling
TRAINS

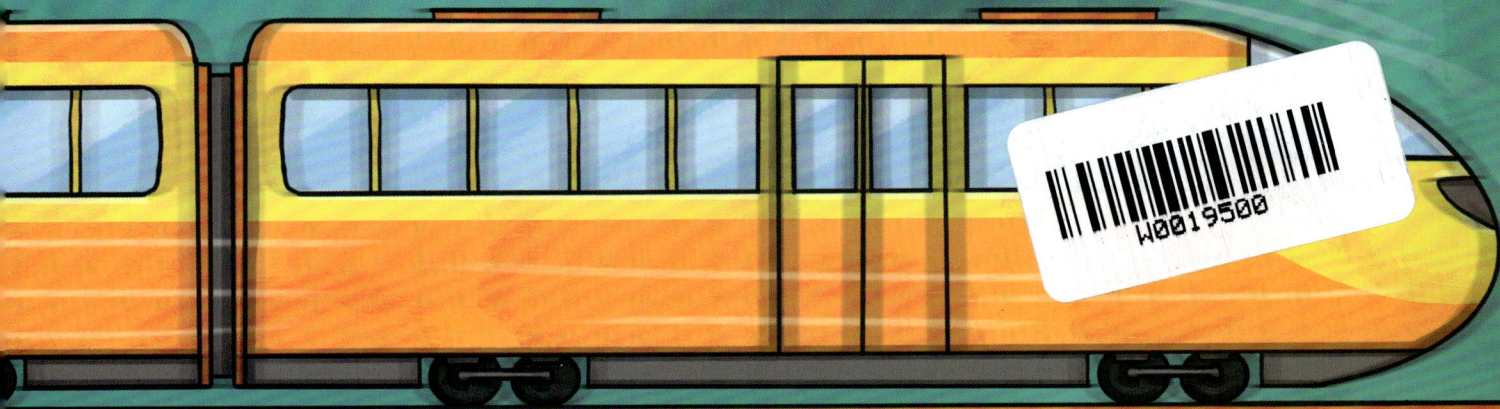

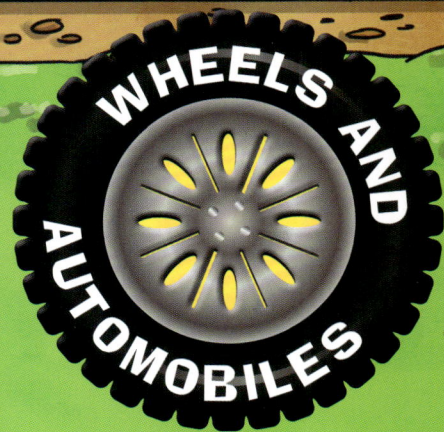

WHEELS AND AUTOMOBILES

FOX EYE
PUBLISHING

A train is a truly tremendous machine
that moves on tracks over land.

Through cities and forests. Past mountains and farms. A trip by train is grand.

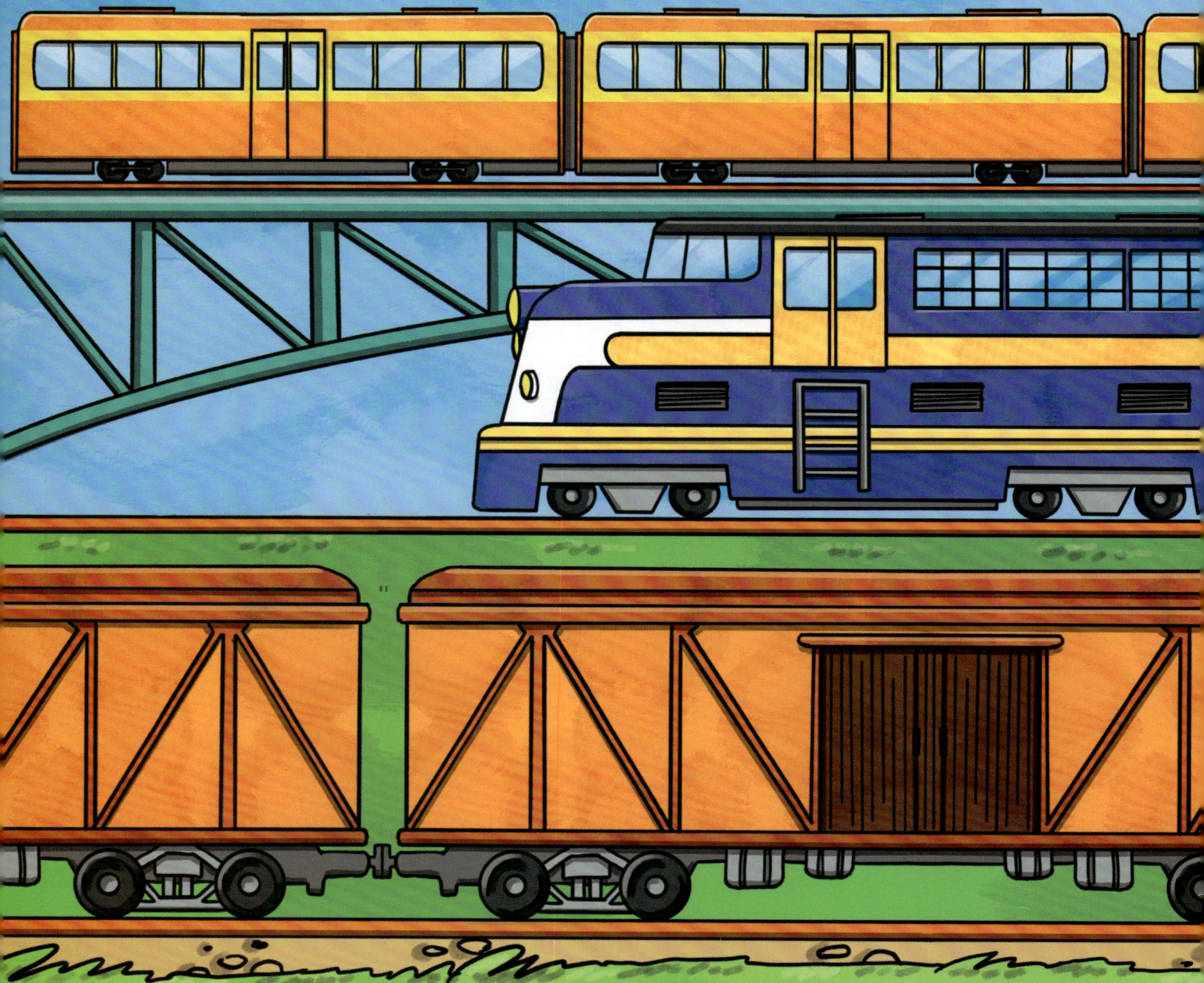

Some can climb mountains. Some go underground.
Trains carry goods and people around.

goods

Can you count the trains in this picture?
How many have you found?

carriage

wheels

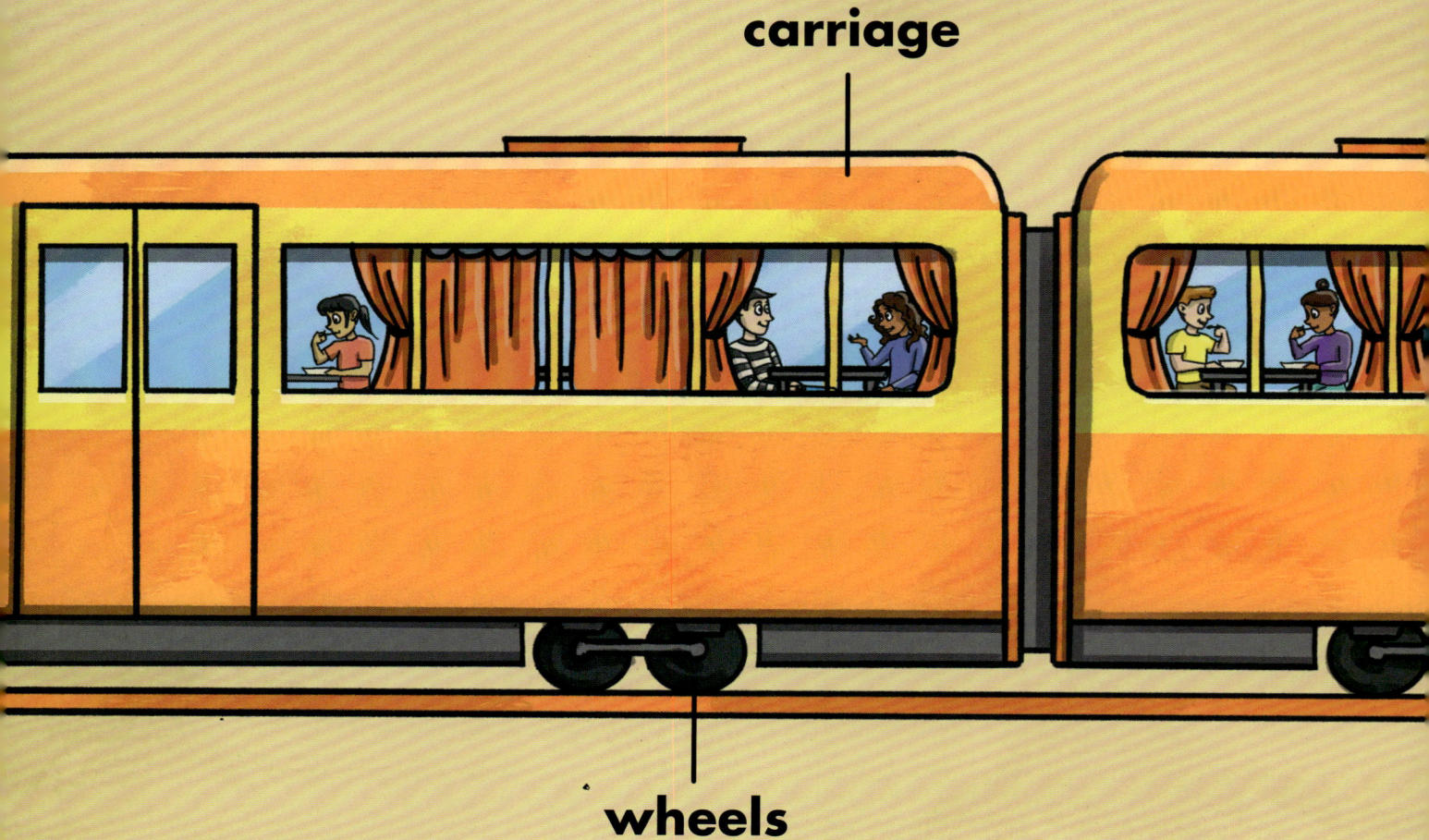

Trains have wagons for carrying goods
or carriages where people relax.

track

The wheels of a train have special grooves.
The grooves keep the train on the tracks.

locomotive

At the front of this freight train is a locomotive. It pulls the wagons along.

wagon

A diesel engine gives the locomotive power.
The engine is very strong.

These wagons are called flatcars. They carry
loads that are bulky and large in size.

Some flatbeds carry containers.
The containers have goods inside.

electric cable

Some passenger trains have electric cables overhead.
Some trains have an electric track, instead.

The electricity gives the train power to move.
Electric trains are quiet and smooth.

The conductor is in charge of the train.
When the passengers are safely inside,

conductor

The conductor blows a whistle to tell the driver it's safe to drive.

Passenger trains have rows of seats
and a narrow central aisle.

Commuter trains have a wider aisle, and the passengers sit or stand at each side.

restaurant

passenger

Here comes an overnight passenger train.
It has restaurants and cabins with beds.

cab

While the passengers sleep, the driver in the cab keeps the train moving full speed ahead.

It is morning now. The sun has come up.
The train travelled through the night.

The train has arrived in its beautiful destination.
The passengers wake and alight.

Bustling Words

Alight means to get off something.

A **cab** is the part of a vehicle in which the driver sits.

A **cabin** is a part of a train in which people sleep.

The **conductor** is in charge of the train.

A **destination** is the place a person travels to.

An **electric cable** is a cable, or piece of wire, through which electricity runs.

Electricity is a type of energy.

An **engine** is part of a vehicle in which energy is made.

A **flatbed** is a flat wagon. It can carry large and heavy loads.

A **freight train** is a train that carries only goods.

A **locomotive** is the part of a train that contains the engine.

A **machine** is something that helps us to do work.

Power is energy to do work.

Tracks are lengths of metal on which trains travel.

Wagons are parts of trains in which things are carried.

First published in 2024 by Fox Eye Publishing
Unit 31, Vulcan House Business Centre,
Vulcan Road, Leicester, LE5 3EF
www.foxeyepublishing.com

Author: Katherine Eason
Art director: Paul Phillips
Cover designer: Emma Bailey
Editor: Jenny Rush

All illustrations by Eszter Szepvolgyi

978-1-80445-345-2

Printed in China